Michel Lescay Arias
Luis Alberto Montoya Acosta

HA High Availability Cluster at Proxmox

Michel Lescay Arias
Luis Alberto Montoya Acosta

HA High Availability Cluster at Proxmox

Sustainability for network services in enterprises

ScienciaScripts

Imprint
Any brand names and product names mentioned in this book are subject to trademark, brand or patent protection and are trademarks or registered trademarks of their respective holders. The use of brand names, product names, common names, trade names, product descriptions etc. even without a particular marking in this work is in no way to be construed to mean that such names may be regarded as unrestricted in respect of trademark and brand protection legislation and could thus be used by anyone.

Cover image: www.ingimage.com

This book is a translation from the original published under ISBN 978-620-0-05290-2.

Publisher:
Sciencia Scripts
is a trademark of
Dodo Books Indian Ocean Ltd. and OmniScriptum S.R.L publishing group

120 High Road, East Finchley, London, N2 9ED, United Kingdom
Str. Armeneasca 28/1, office 1, Chisinau MD-2012, Republic of Moldova, Europe
Printed at: see last page
ISBN: 978-620-7-12188-5

High Availability (HA) cluster on Proxmox 5.1

Lic. Michel Lescay Arias

Luis Alberto Montoya Acosta

TABLE OF CONTENTS:

Introduction

ICTs have burst into our lives thanks to the Internet. When we talk about new technologies applied to medicine, education, commerce or leisure, we are referring, to a large extent, to the use of the Internet in any of these areas.

Most of the services we access on the internet are supported on cloud servers and virtualisation tools. It is important to know from theory what virtualisation is according to Ali Susandri and Rahmaddeni in 2015 "technology designed to provide a layer of abstraction between the hardware of computer equipment and the software that runs on them".

By virtualisation platform we mean a structure composed of different services that manage multiple virtualisation technologies. They integrate storage subsystems, networks and virtual machines in the same environment, centralising and simplifying their management. They are tools for the virtualisation of complete data centres and make up the existing reality under the concept of the cloud. Thanks to their development, the infrastructure as a service (IaaS) business model has emerged, in which providers maintain the hardware and rent servers, storage space and networks (all virtualised) to their clients.

The idea of this project arises from the need of the community of health professionals in Santiago de Cuba to have professional blogs, institutional websites, discussion forums, cloud, as well as other web services necessary in today's world for any professional with fault tolerance that allows systems to continue providing services.

To carry out this project, we will use virtualisation systems that are little known by the professional community outside Information and Communications Technology, but which have now grown as an alternative to the giants that dominate the market.

Since the main purpose is to achieve sustainability in the services provided by the Provincial Health Node in Santiago de Cuba to its professionals, it was determined after analysing and carrying out numerous tests that the objective would be achieved with three **Proxmox** servers, with the **cluster** created between them, and, within one of them, a virtual machine with **Debian 8**, **Apache** and WordPress as a basic hosting service for blogs and websites, so that if the server containing the virtual machine fails, it will migrate to another server and can continue to function. In addition, we will have to have an external virtual machine configured in Debian 8, with a shared **NFS** storage implemented in which the Proxmox virtual machine is stored for its correct functioning.

CHAPTER 1

Proxmox

Proxmox Virtual Environment is an open source server virtualisation environment that is 100% free and unlimited in its use. It is a Debian-based Linux distribution that enables the deployment and management of virtual machines and containers. It includes a web console and command line tools, and provides a REST API for third-party tools.

PROXMOX VE offers similar benefits to virtualisation products such as VMware vSphere, Windows Hyper-V, Citrix XenServer and others.

The official website of this environment or virtualisation tool is: https://www.proxmox.com

As PROXMOX is free at no cost, you can install it on any number of "physical servers", with no limit on processor and socket usage, communication bridges, or NAS or SAN integration either via Fibre Channel, iSCSI over Ethernet or NFS.

Here are the features of Proxmox:

1. **HTML5 Web Manager**. PROXMOX provides a Web interface to configure physical servers, clusters, virtual machines, backup policies, restore backups, snapshots. It is not necessary to install client applications on your machine to manage and being HTML5 allows you to connect and manage the virtualised environment from your Android Smartphone, Iphone, tablet's, among others.

2. **Virtualisation for most Operating Systems**, in their 32/64bit versions: Linux in all its versions, Microsoft Windows 10 / 2016 / 2012 / 7 / 8/ 2003 /xp, Solaris, AIX, among others.

3. **KVM (Kernel-based Virtual Machine)** is a solution for implementing virtualisation on Linux. It can run on x86/x86_64 hardware and requires the microprocessor to have Intel "VT" and on AMD "SVM" virtualisation support.

4. **Container-based Virtualisation (LXC),** is an alternative for running "Linux" machines in separate spaces. Unlike virtualisation, it works as an add-on module to the physical server and makes direct use of the hardware (also known as paravirtualisation).

5. **Backup & Restore of "Virtual Machines"**. Proxmox makes it very easy to perform these tasks and is managed through its web interface. You can perform a backup immediately or leave it scheduled. Restoring is simple, just select the backup to restore and that's it.

6. **Snapshots Live**. allows you to make snapshots of "Virtual Machines" including the contents of RAM, their configuration and the state of virtual disks. You can roll back in time the "Virtual Machine" by restoring spanshot's.

7. **Hot migration"**. The left graph shows a small cluster consisting of 3 nodes and populated with "Virtual Machines". A node with an overload is shown with a red background. The administration of the nodes is centralised through a web interface, allowing you to move "Virtual Machines" between each "Physical Server (Node)" without having to shut down the "Virtual Machine".

8. **Network Bridges.** Proxmox manages the physical cards through "Bridges" that it shares with

the "Virtual Machines". It is very easy to associate 1 or several cards to a Bridge, automatically balancing the data traffic.

Proxmox 5.1

We decided to use Proxmox in its 5.1 version because of the experience I have accumulated in 5 years working with this environment and because it is a very complete virtualisation tool. We can affirm this by showing the main new features of this update:

- The base operating system used by Proxmox is based on Debian 9.2 "Stretch".
- It includes Linux Kernel 4.13 and ZFS for storage.
- Ceph v12.2 Luminous is a stable version of this software-based storage solution that allows us to have much greater control over our entire storage system.

2.1 Installation requirements

On the official Proxmox website, a series of minimum and recommended requirements for installation are detailed. These requirements are as follows:

Hadware	Minimum	Recommended
CPU	64 bit (Intel EMT64 or AMD64)	64 bit (Intel EMT64 or AMD64)
Processor	Intel VT / AMD-V with KVM virtualisation support	Intel VT / AMD-V with KVM virtualisation support
RAM	1 GB	8 GB
Hard Disk	Normal hard disk	Hard disk with 15k rpm speed. RAID recommended
Network cards	A	Two or more

Table 1. Proxmox requirements comparison

Later we will show a network diagram of the infrastructure to be used in this project for a better understanding of it and you will also be able to see all the data that we will use in the configuration of the equipment.

CHAPTER 2

Basic concepts

In order to understand more accurately the importance of this project, it is necessary to offer some elements of vital importance in order to achieve the purposes of this project.

The first concept that needs to be clarified is that of **cluster**, commonly the term cluster is applied to sets or clusters of computers (servers) linked together usually by a high-speed network and behaving as if they were a single computer. They are usually employed to improve performance and/or availability.

The second concept to clarify is that of **high availability (HA),** HA is a system design protocol and its associated implementation that ensures a certain absolute degree of operational continuity during a given measurement period. Availability refers to the ability of the user community to access the system, services offered by providers, undertake new work, update existing work and collect the results of previously performed work.

The last concept that is important to know is that of a high availability cluster, which is a set of two or more machines that are characterised by maintaining a series of shared services and by constantly monitoring each other.

There are two kinds of high availability, in this case ours is going to be that, if there is a hardware or application failure on any of the machines in the cluster, the high availability software is able to automatically start the services that have failed on any of the other machines in the cluster. And when the failed machine recovers, the services are migrated back to the original machine.

CHAPTER 3

Project structure

In order to develop our project and so that all those who consult this material have greater clarity when it comes to executing it with physical professional servers, I offer you the data that we will use throughout the process of creating the High Availability Cluster with Proxmox 5.1. For this we will have four virtual machines, three of them will form the Proxmox cluster and the other machine will be the shared storage server using NFS.

To run this infrastructure, we will use the virtualisation software **VMWare Workstation**, below, we detail the information needed to run the project.

	Proxmox 1	Proxmox 2	Proxmox 23	NFS
Name	prox1.michelpress.co m	prox2.michelpress.co m	prox3.michelpress.com	nfs.michelpress. com
IP	192.168.1.2	192.168.1.3	192.168.1.4	192.168.1.10
RAM	1 GB	1 GB	1 GB	2 GB
Hard Disk	25 GB	25 GB	25 GB	50 GB
Network Interface	One (with bridging adapter)	One (with bridging adapter)	One (with bridging adapter)	One (with bridging adapter)
OS version	Proxmox VE 5.1	Proxmox VE 5.1	Proxmox VE 5.1	Debian 8.8

Table 2. Project structure

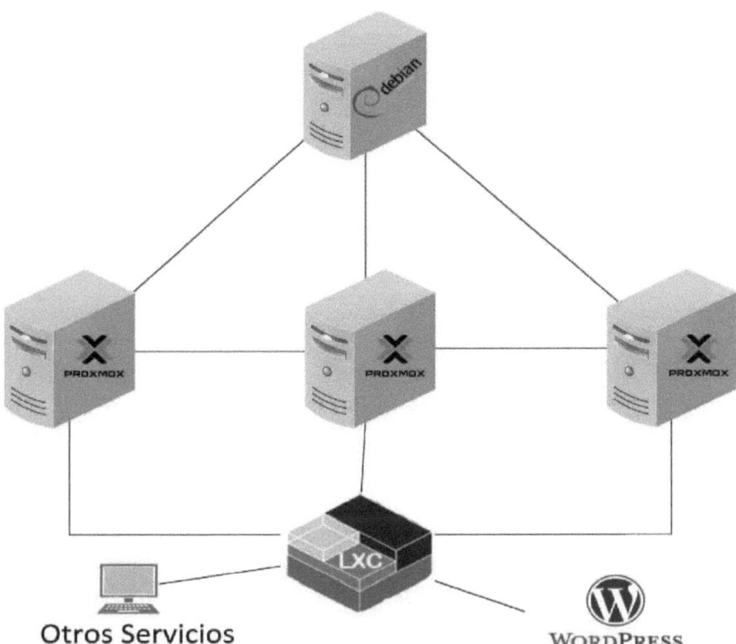

Figure 1. Project network diagram. 1

To access the servers we will use a VNC connection provided by the Proxmox interface itself and also, if necessary, we will use SSH clients such as Putty or MobaXterm.

CHAPTER 4

Installation of Proxmox 5.1

To begin installing the servers in virtual machines, we download the virtualisation software VMWare Workstation Pro 12, which we download from its official website, and then we install it: https://www.vmware.com/go/downloadworkstation

We will start with the Proxmox server prox1.michelpress.com. The first thing we have to do is to open our virtualisation software VMWare Workstation Pro 12 and create a new virtual machine.

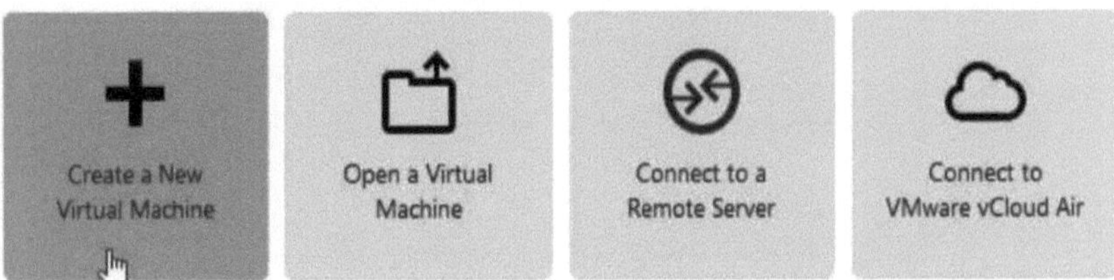

Figure 2. Proxmox Server 1, 1

After doing the previous action, a window will pop up to choose what type of configuration our virtual machine will have, leave the option recommended by the software and click on Next.

Figure 2. Proxmox Server 1, 2

Next, we choose the downloaded Proxmox 5.1 ISO image file on our PC.

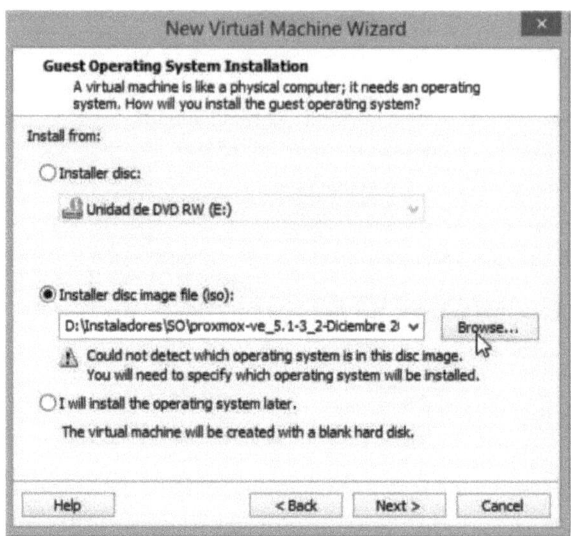

Figure 2. Proxmox Server 1, 3

Now, we select the type of OS (Operating System) and its version (distribution and CPU type (32 or 64 bit)). In our case we will select the Linux System and 64 bit Architecture. These are compatible with Proxmox 5.1. It is important that the motherboard we use has the possibility of virtualisation for 32 and 64 bit. This can be configured in the BIOS of our PC.

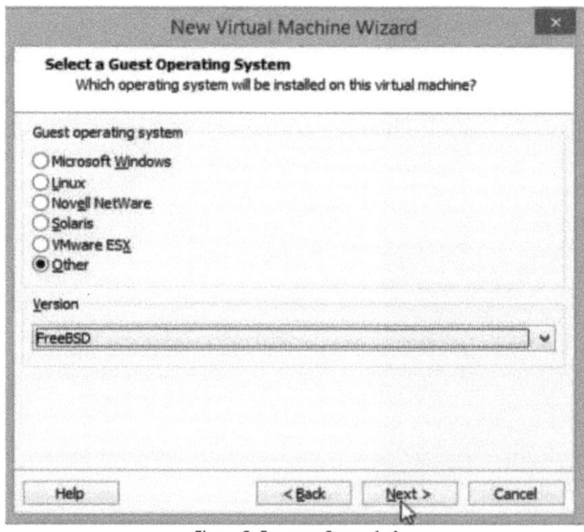

Figure 2. Proxmox Server 1, 4

We continue by declaring the name and the place where our virtual machines are stored during the execution of the project.

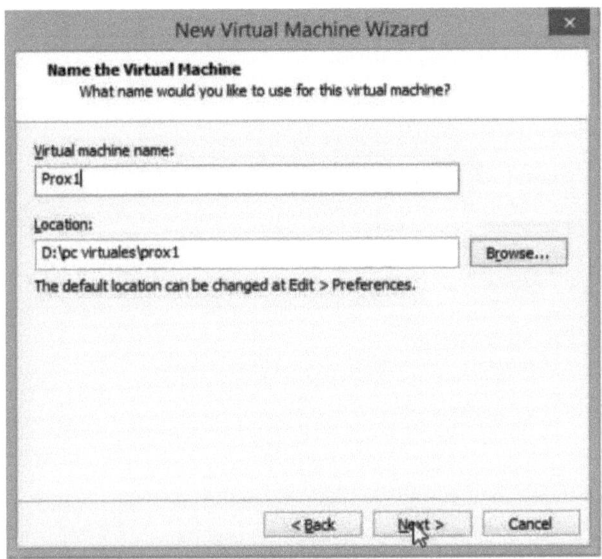

Figure 2. Proxmox Server 1, 5

We choose the disk size we have defined in table 2 and the storage type of our virtual machine.

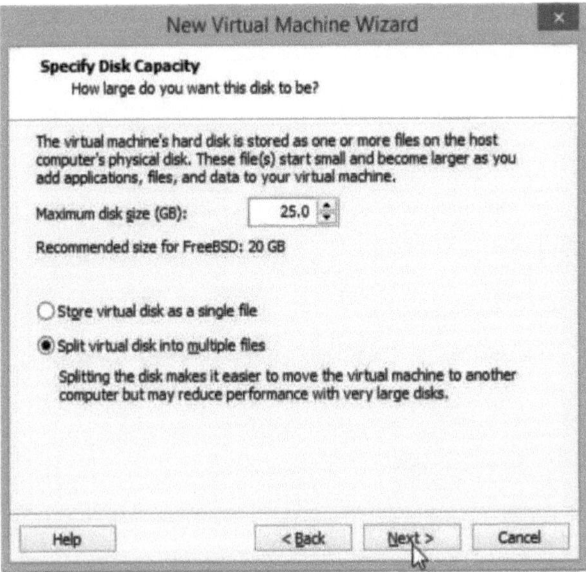

Figure 2. Proxmox Server 1, 6

Pressing *Next* displays a window with a summary of the characteristics and attributes of our virtual machine.

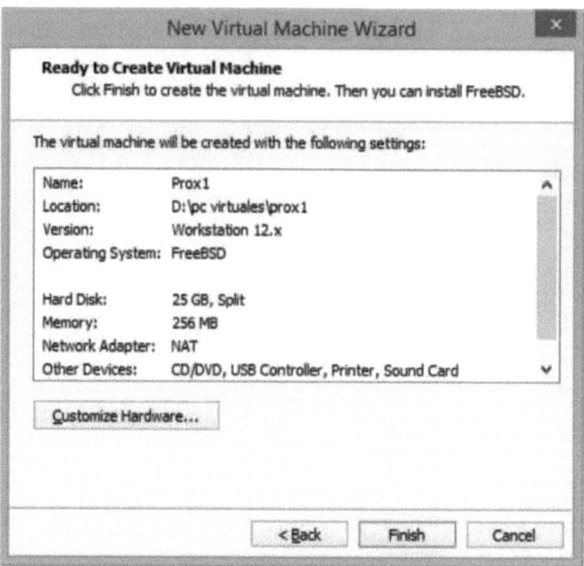

Figure 2. Proxmox Server 1, 7

Here we will adjust the RAM of our Virtual PC as we declared that it would have 1024 Mbps (1 GB). Click on *Customize Hardware* and add the necessary amount so that our Proxmox 5.1 system works with the highest possible quality.

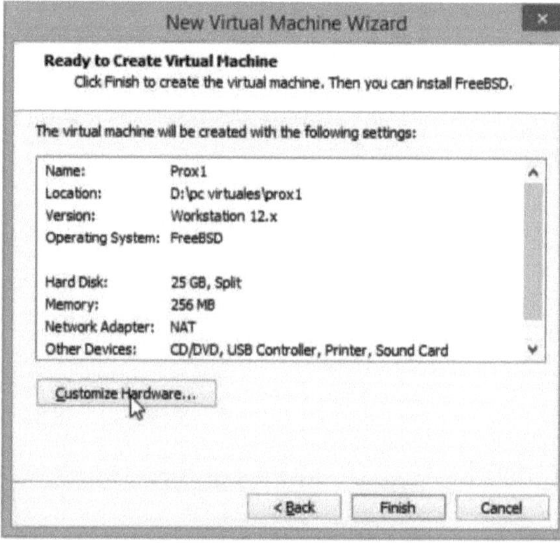

Figure 2. Proxmox Server 1, 8

Click on *Close and* the last step to create our virtual machine is to press *Finish*.

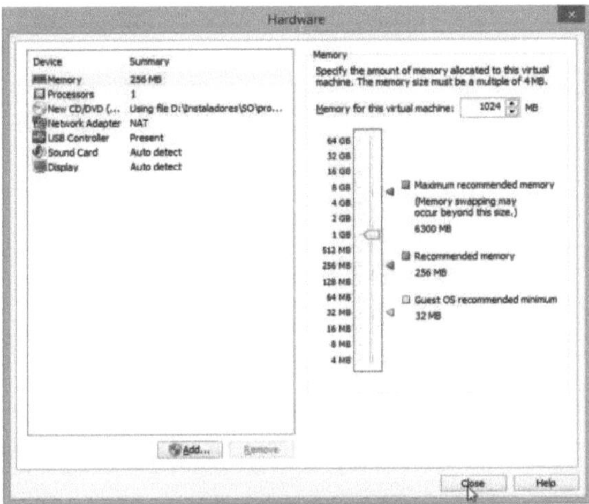

Figure 2. Proxmox Server 1, 9

To achieve communication between our virtual machines and the host OS, we will have to configure the network of all the machines in bridge mode. To do this, go to the *Network Adapter* section of *Customize Hardware* and change the type of adapter connection.

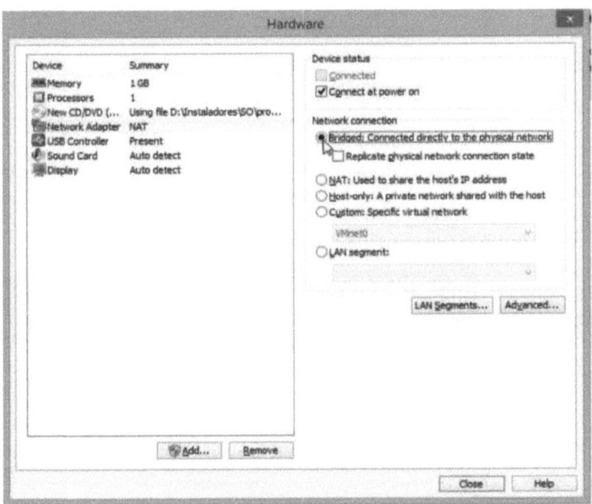

Figure 2. Proxmox Server 1, 10

Next, we proceed to start the virtual machine that we have created with our Proxmox 5.1.

Figure 2. proxmox server 1, 11

When starting the virtual machine, the initial Proxmox 5.1 installation screen will appear. Click on the first option.

Figure 2. proxmox server 1, 12

We accept the Proxmox license terms to continue with the installation.

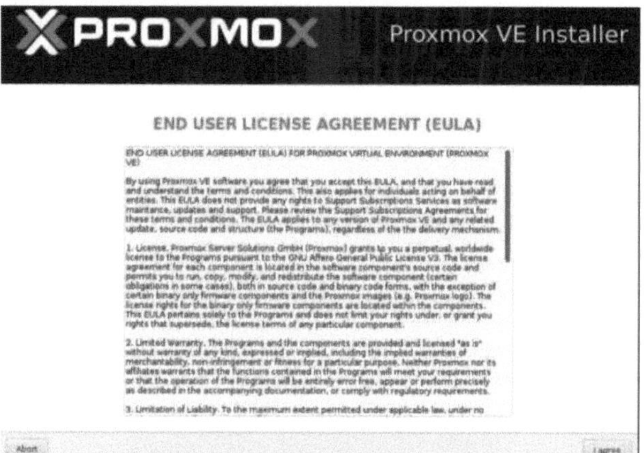

Figure 2. proxmox Server 1, 13

Now we select the disk where we will install the system and press *Next*.

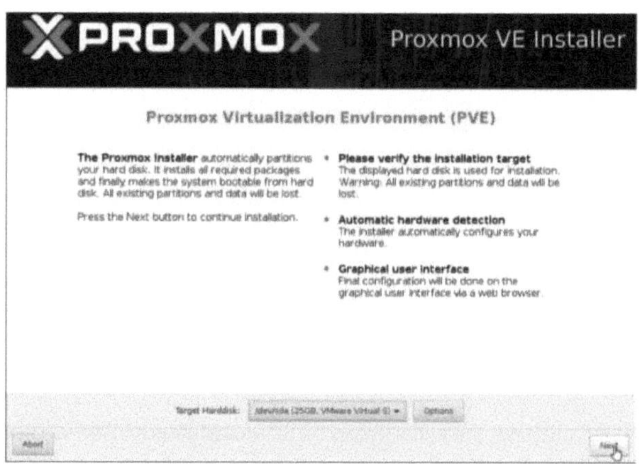

Figure 2. proxmox server 1, 14

Next, we enter our location (Country) and Time Zone and Proxmox Keyboard Language and click *Next*.

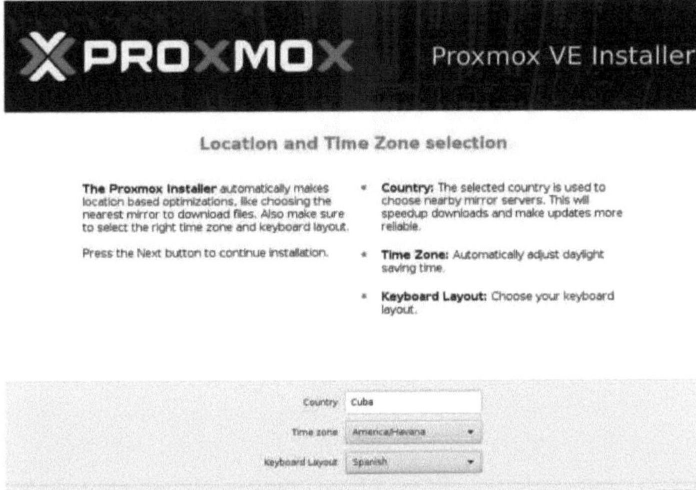

Figure 2. proxmox server 1, 15

Next, we will need to enter a password for the server and an email address to which alerts will be sent in case of server errors.

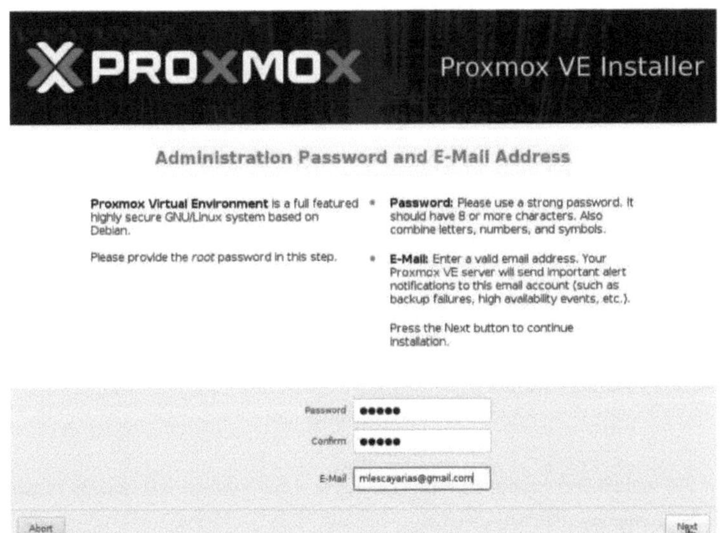

Figure 2. proxmox server 1, 16

To conclude with the data before starting the installation of the system, we must assign the data to the server according to table 2 of this document.

Hostname (FQDN):
prox1.michelpress.com

IP Address:
192.168.1.2

Netmask:
255.255.255.0

Gateway: 192.168.1.1

DNS Server:

192.168.1.1

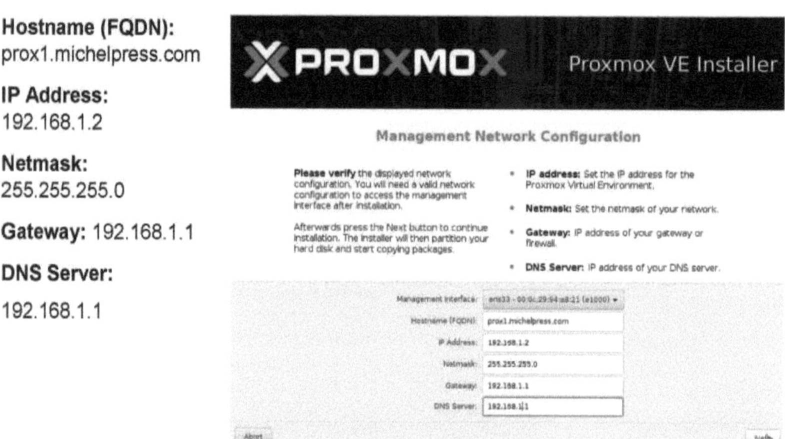

Figure 2. proxmox server 1, 17

Once the above steps have been completed, the proxmox 5.1 installation process will begin.

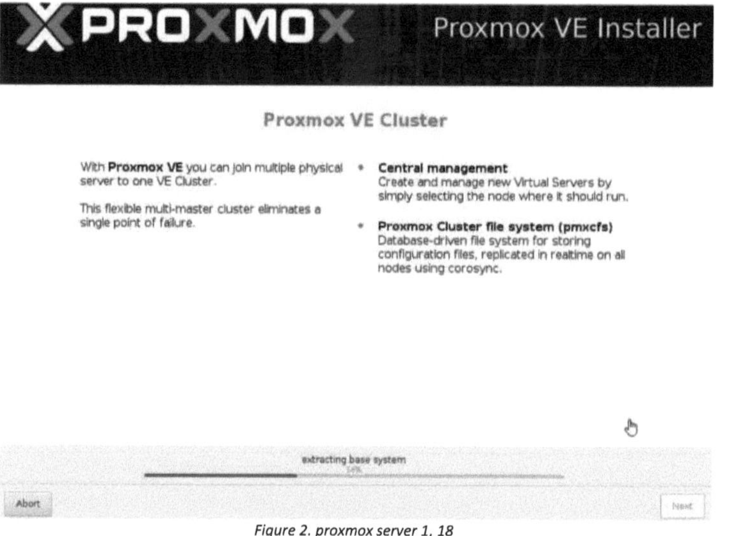

Figure 2. proxmox server 1, 18

At the end of the installation process press *Reboot* and the system will quickly restart, eject the installation media either by CD/DVD or USB.

Figure 2. proxmox server 1, 19

When restarting the server, you will be able to log in with a username and password (root and the previously assigned password). On this Proxmox server, configurations can be made via the console and also via the proxmox web interface. You can access it via a Windows computer that is connected to the same network segment as the Proxmox server and the following image provides you with the necessary information to access the web interface:

Figura 2.   proxmox server 1, 20

To show you what is explained in the previous paragraph, we are going to launch a browser (the one of your choice). Once inside Firefox, type in the IP and the port (8006) where the Proxmox web interface listens. Change the language to Spanish and enter the user(root) and password (the same as for accessing the console).

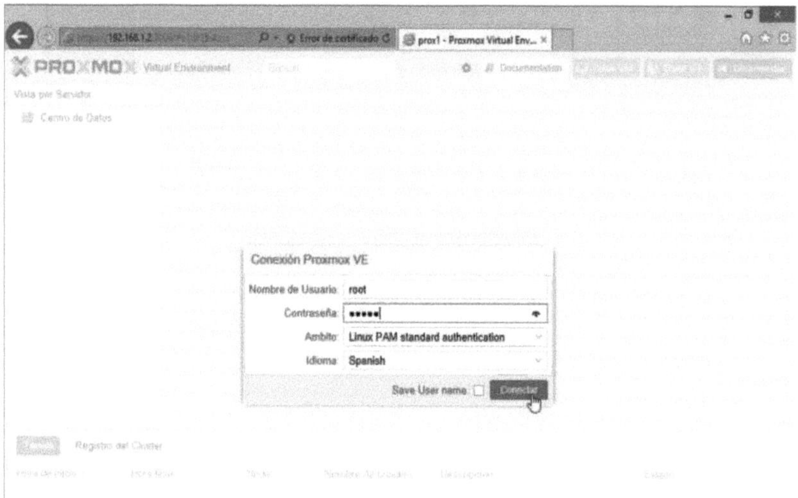

Figure 2. proxmox server 1, 21

Figure 2. proxmox server 1, 22

Next we will perform the same steps of installation, configuration and testing of the proxmox console and web interface for the prox2.michelpress.com and prox3.michelpress.com servers. In order not to repeat the information we will only show the network configuration for both servers.

For the prox2.michelpress.com server, we insert the following data in the network configuration:

Hostname(FQDN):
prox2.michelpress.com

IP Address:
192.168.1.3

Netmask:
255.255.255.0

Gateway: 192.168.1.1

DNS Server:
192.168.1.1

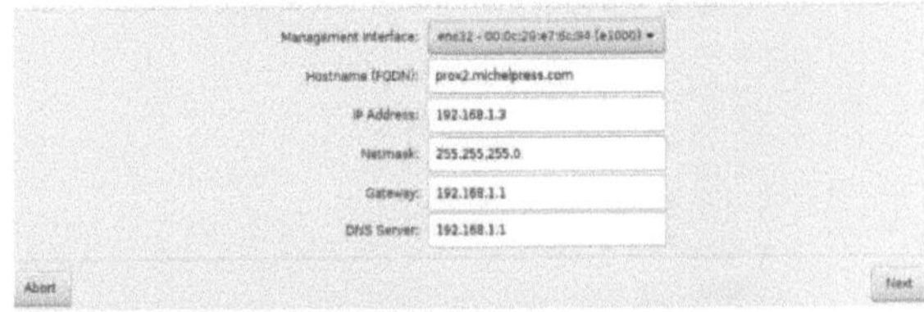

Figure 3. Proxmox Server 2, 1

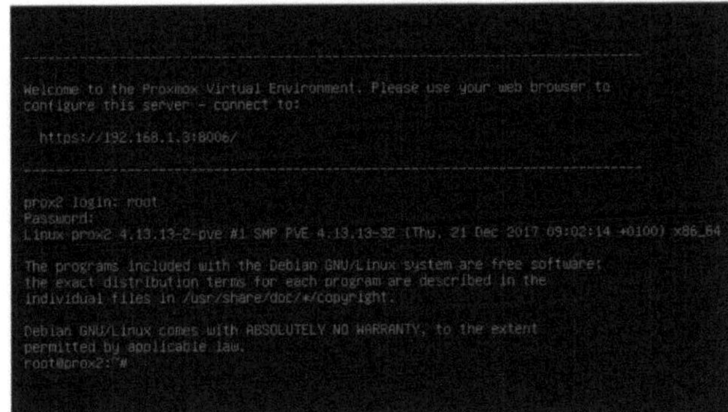

Figura 3.   Proxmox Server 2, 2

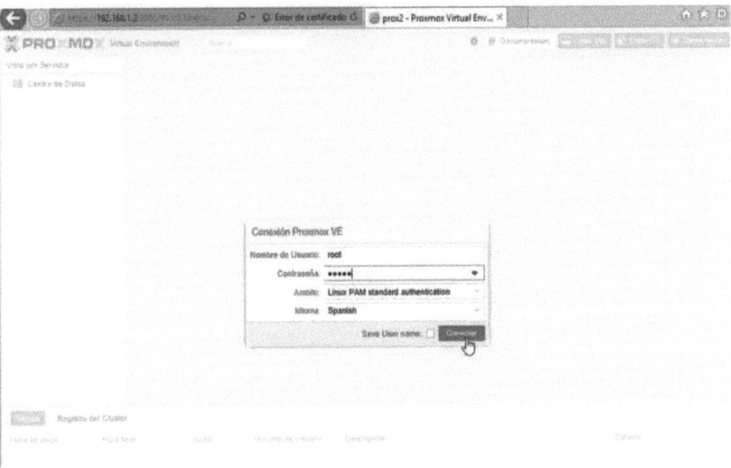

Figure 3. Proxmox Server 2, 3

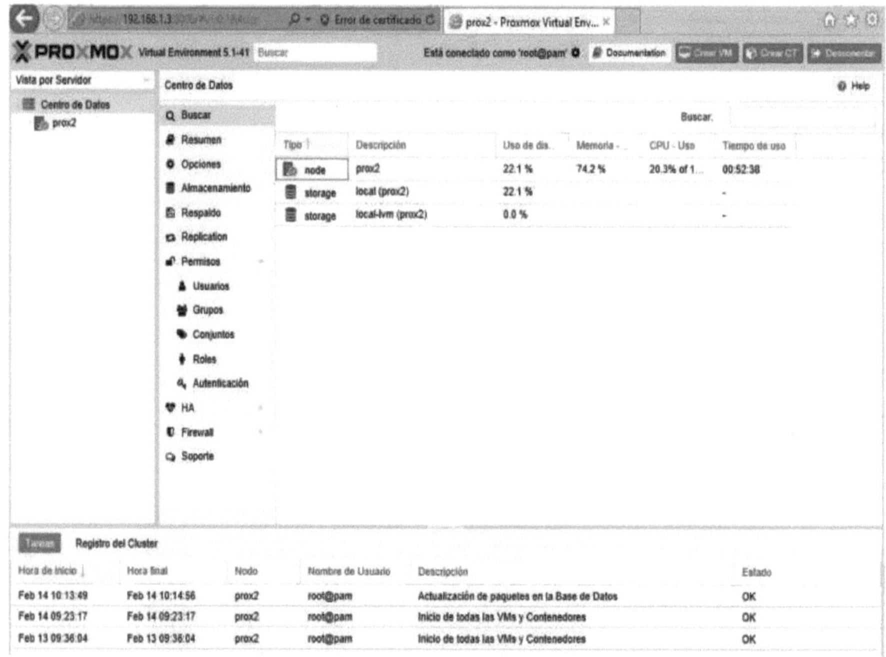

Figura 3.   Proxmox Server 2, 4

For the prox3.michelpress.com server, we insert the following data in the network configuration:

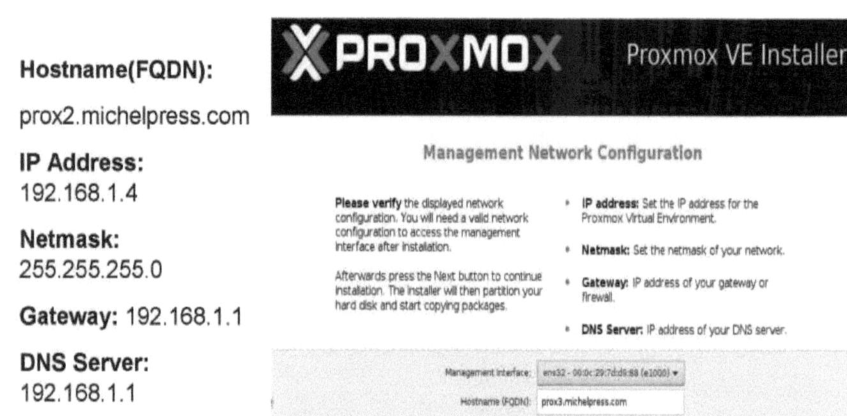

Figura 4.   Proxmox Server 3, 1

Welcome to the Proxmox Virtual Environment. Please use your web browser to
configure this server - connect to:

  https://192.168.1.4:8006/

prox3 login: root
Password:
Linux prox3 4.13.13-2-pve #1 SMP PVE 4.13.13-32 (Thu, 21 Dec 2017 09:02:14 +0100) x86_64

The programs included with the Debian GNU/Linux system are free software;
the exact distribution terms for each program are described in the
individual files in /usr/share/doc/*/copyright.

Debian GNU/Linux comes with ABSOLUTELY NO WARRANTY, to the extent
permitted by applicable law.
root@prox3:~#

Figura 4.   Proxmox Server 3, 2

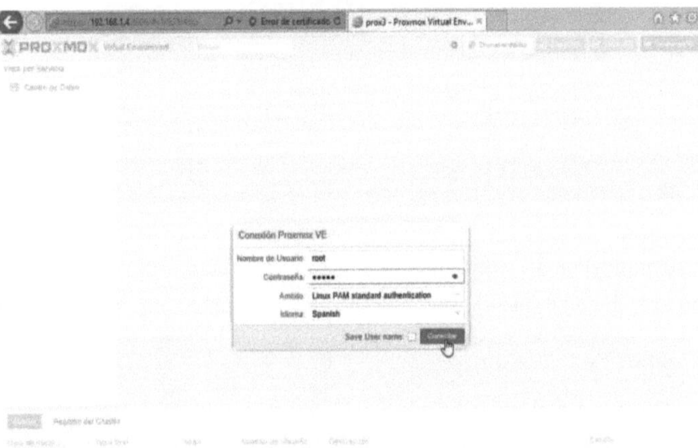

Figure 4. Proxmox Server 3, 3

Figure 4. Proxmox Server 3, 4

Every time we start our proxmox server through the web interface we are presented with the following window. All we have to do is click on the "Ok" option.

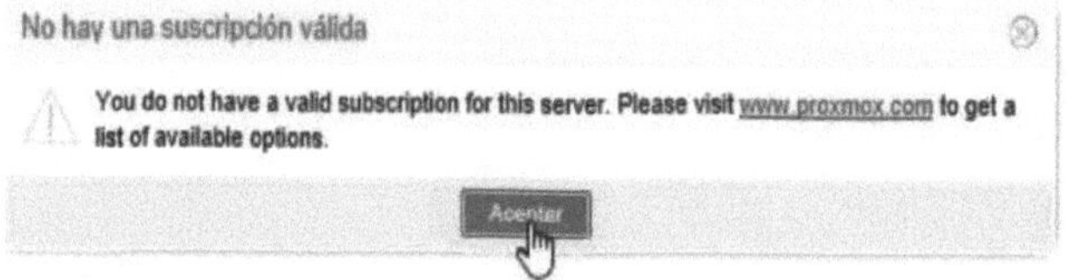

Figure 5. Invalid subscription, 1

If you want to remove this window, you must execute the steps that I will explain below. These steps apply in the same way for all 3 servers. We go to the directory /usr/share/pve-manager/js with the command cd

Figure 5. Invalid subscription, 2

Next, we edit the pvemanagerlib.js file with our preferred text editor, in this case I will do it with nano.

```
root@prox1:/usr/share/pve-manager/js# nano pvemanagerlib.js
```

Figure 5. Invalid subscription, 3

We locate line 510 approximately which looks like this: if (data.status !== 'Active') {
We comment the above, add if (false) { and it would look like in the figure below

```
//if (data.status !== 'Active') {
if (false) {
                    Ext.Msg.show({
                        title: gettext('No valid subscription'),
                        icon: Ext.Msg.WARNING,
                        msg: PVE.Utils.noSubKeyHtml,
                        buttons: Ext.Msg.OK,
                        callback: function(btn) {
                            if (btn !== 'ok') {
                                return;
                            }
                            orig_cmd();
                        }
                    });
                } else {
                    orig_cmd();
                }
            });
        },
```

Figura 5.   Invalid subscription, 4

We save the changes, visit our web interface and refresh our browser several times with Ctrl + F5 to jump out of the browser.

CHAPTER 5

Installing NFS shared storage

Once the 3 Proxmox 5.1 servers are installed, we will start installing the NFS shared storage server. This will be in charge of storing the virtual machines that we will create in our Proxmox servers.

The procedure to create the virtual machine in VMWare Workstation Pro 12 is the same, just change the hardware configuration and the ISO we will use. In this case we will use the Debian 8.8 Linux distribution.

When starting the virtual machine, the installation process begins with the initial Debian 8 screen.

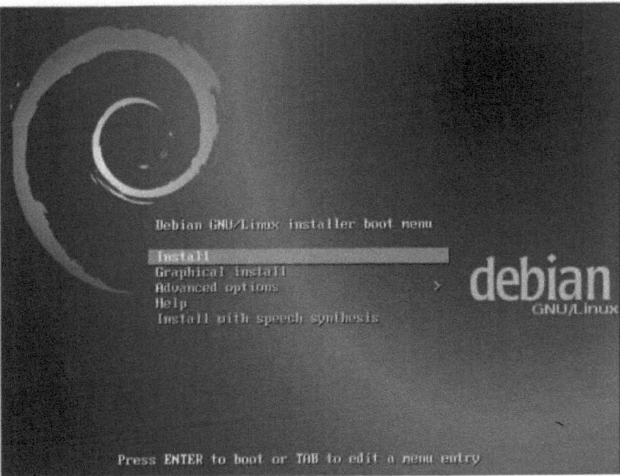

Figura 6.   NFS storage, 1

We select the system language, locale and keyboard to use on our shared storage server.

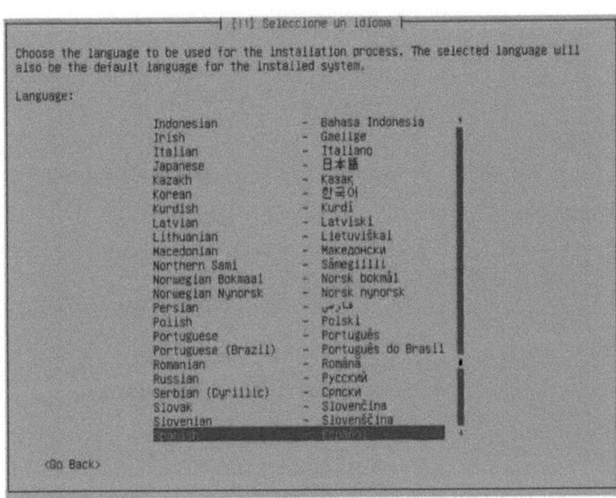

Figura 6.   NFS storage, 2

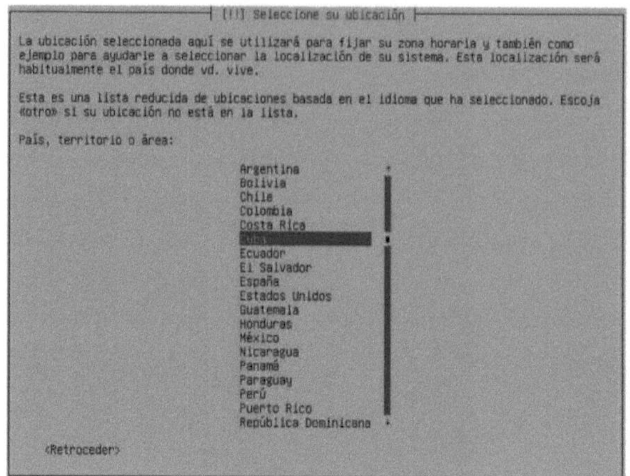

Figure 6. NFS storage, 3

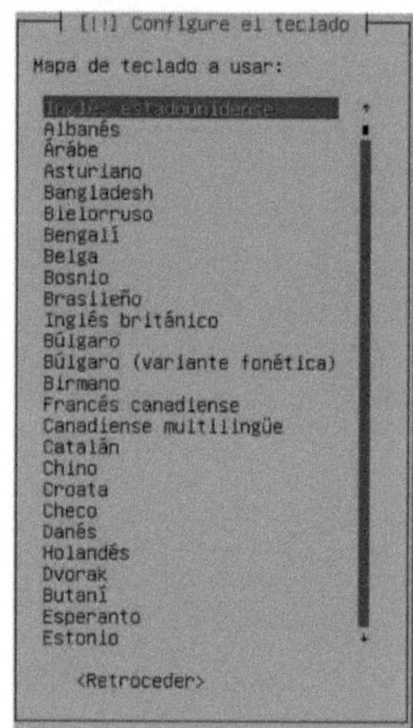

Figure 6. NFS storage, 4

Now the system will try to configure the network automatically (DHCP), otherwise we configure it manually as shown in the following figure:

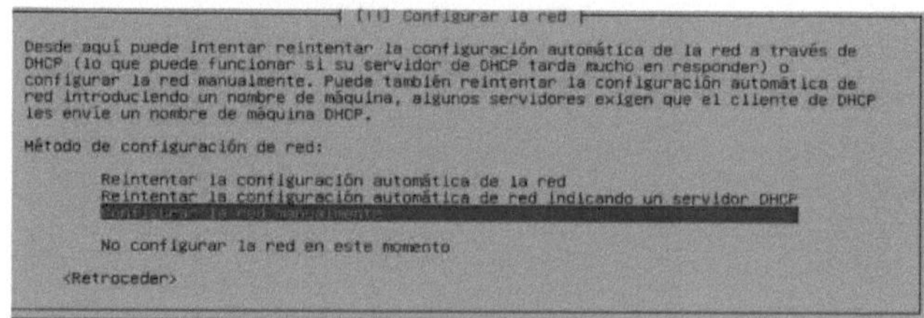

Figure 6. NFS storage, 5

In the following figures we configure the IP address, subnet mask, gateway and DNS.

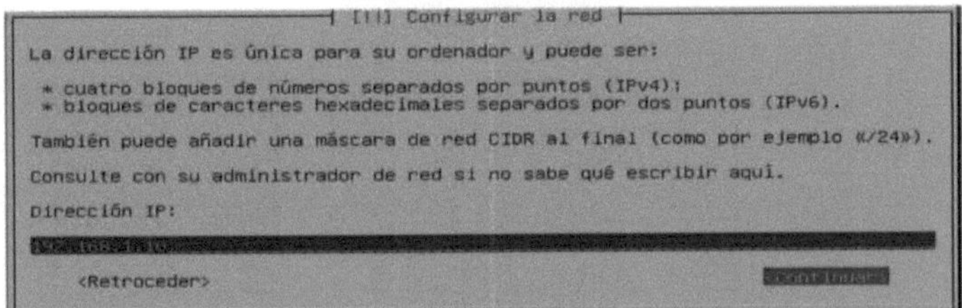

Figure 6. NFS storage, 6

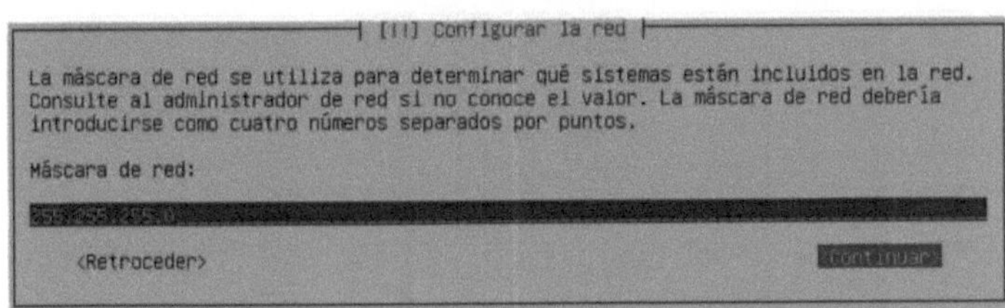

Figure 6. NFS storage, 7

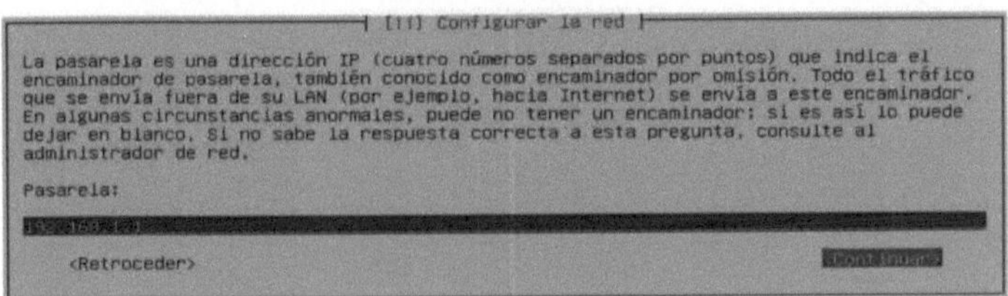

Figure 6. NFS storage, 8

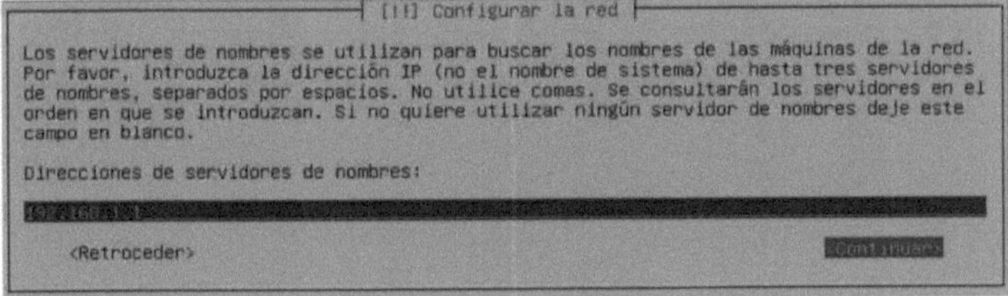

Figure 6. NFS storage, 9

We then declare the machine name, domain, super user password, local user name, password and confirmation.

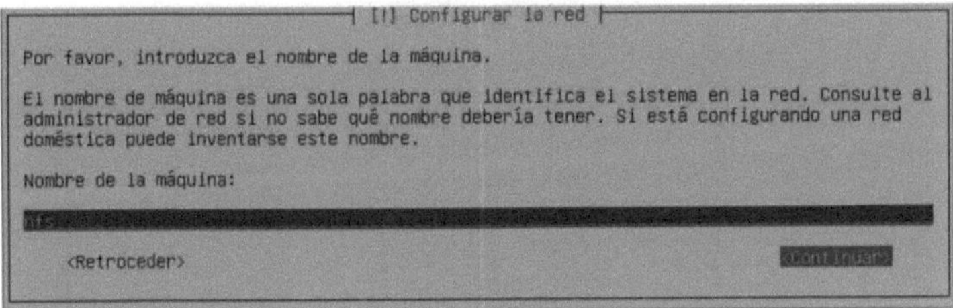

Figure 6. NFS storage, 10

25

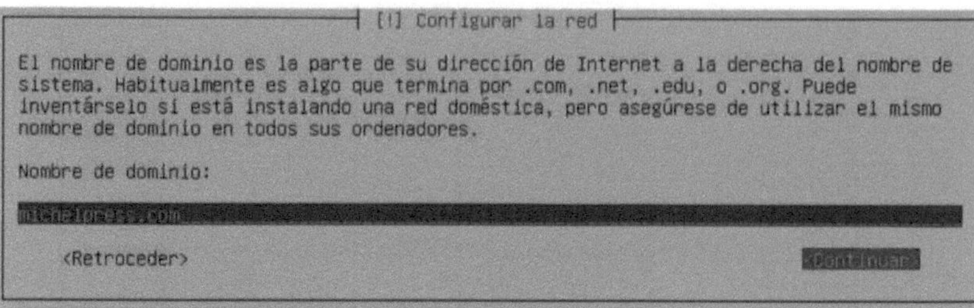

Figure 6. NFS storage, 11

Figure 6. NFS storage, 12

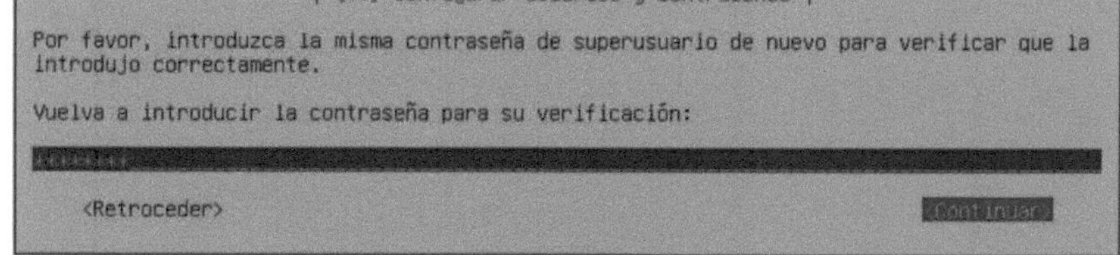

Figure 6. NFS storage, 13

Figure 6. NFS storage, 14

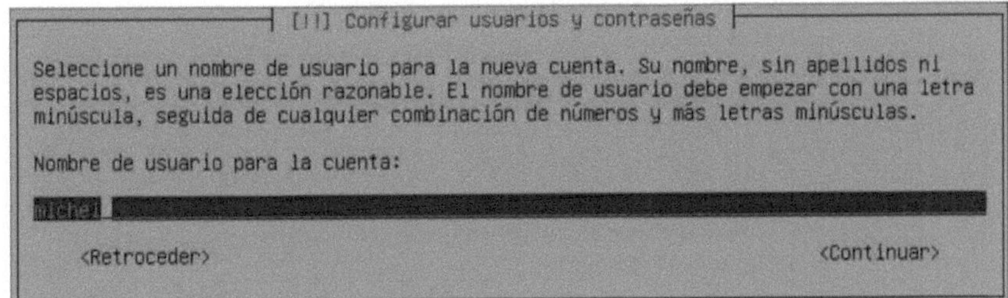

Figure 6. NFS storage, 15

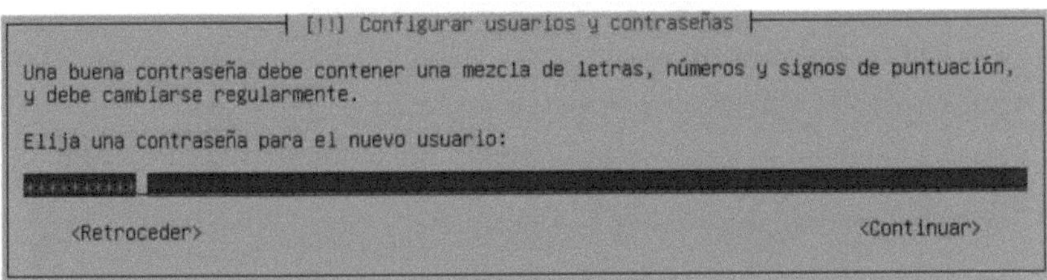

Figure 6. NFS storage, 16

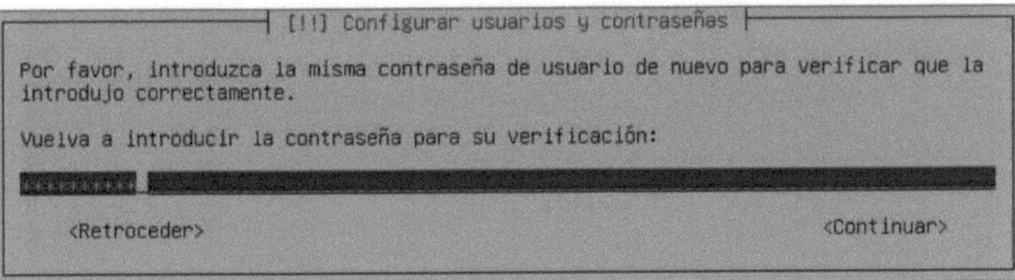

Figure 6. NFS storage, 17

Now we proceed to partition the disk of our NFS server.

Select the option *Guided - use full disk and configure LVM.*

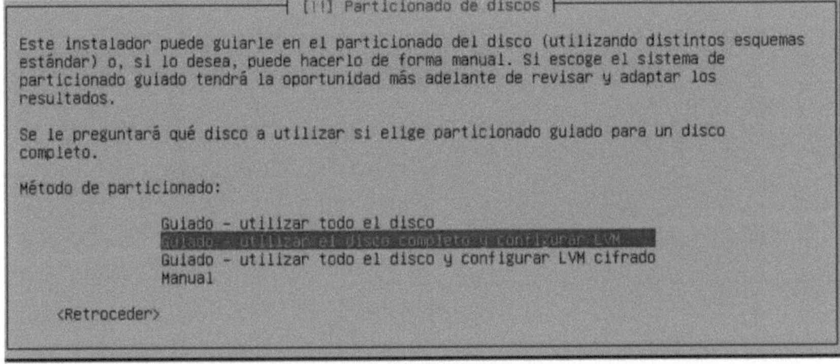

Figure 6. NFS storage, 18

Choose the disk to be partitioned, which in this case is a single disk.

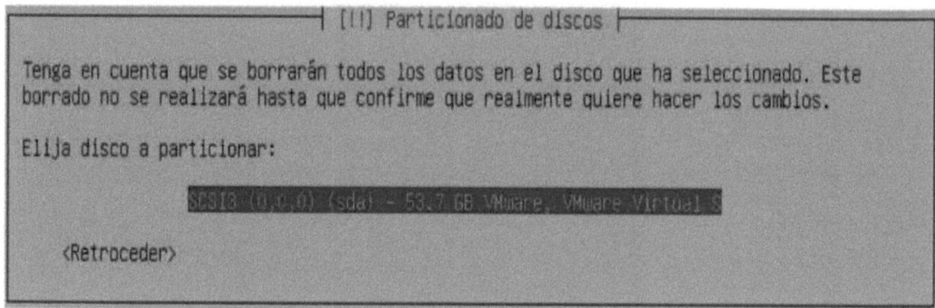

Figure 6. NFS storage, 19

If you are new to Linux partitioning, select the first option, otherwise choose the second or third option according to your needs and confirm when prompted by the installation.

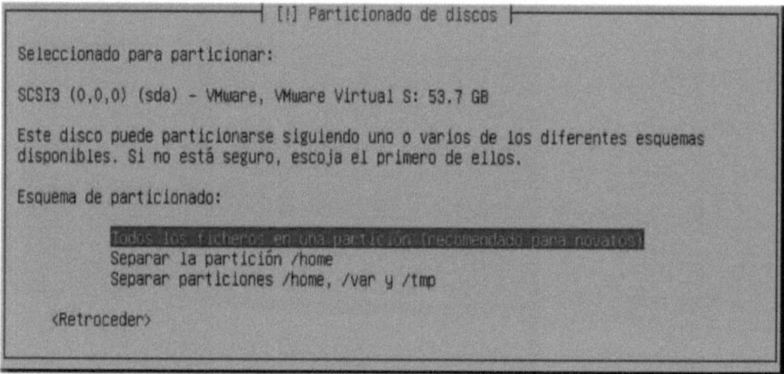

Figure 6. NFS storage, 20

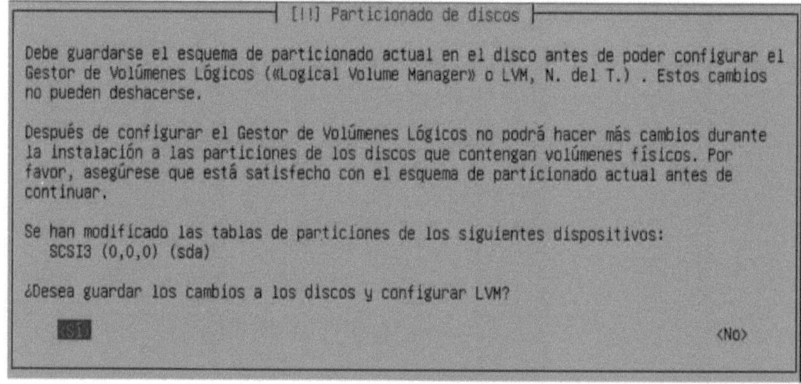

Figure 6. NFS storage, 21

Before starting the installation, we confirm the LVM partitioning changes we have made.

Figure 6. NFS storage, 22

Figure 6. NFS storage, 23

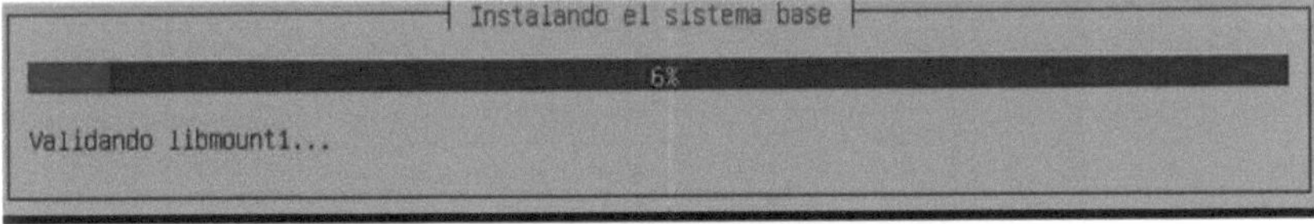

Figure 6. NFS storage, 24

After finishing the installation, we will reboot the server and we will be able to access our Debian 8.8 to proceed to install the NFS server.

Figure 6. NFS storage, 25

Before installing the NFS server we update the packages of the Jessie version of Debian we are using in this project with the command apt-get update.

```
root@nfs:~# apt-get update
Ign http://ftp.sld.cu jessie InRelease
Des:1 http://ftp.sld.cu jessie Release.gpg [2434 B]
Des:2 http://ftp.sld.cu jessie Release [148 kB]
Obj http://ftp.sld.cu jessie/main amd64 Packages
Obj http://ftp.sld.cu jessie/contrib amd64 Packages
Obj http://ftp.sld.cu jessie/non-free amd64 Packages
Des:3 http://ftp.sld.cu jessie/contrib Translation-en [38,3 kB]
Des:4 http://ftp.sld.cu jessie/main Translation-es [314 kB]
Des:5 http://ftp.sld.cu jessie/main Translation-en [4583 kB]
Des:6 http://ftp.sld.cu jessie/non-free Translation-en [72,1 kB]
Descargados 5159 kB en 20s (254 kB/s)
Leyendo lista de paquetes... Hecho
root@nfs:~#
```

Figure 6. NFS storage, 26

After updating the repositories we will install the package containing the NFS service, in this case nfs-kernel-server with the command apt-get install nfs- kernel-server.

```
root@nfs:~# apt-get install nfs-kernel-server
Leyendo lista de paquetes... Hecho
Creando árbol de dependencias
Leyendo la información de estado... Hecho
Se instalarán los siguientes paquetes NUEVOS:
  nfs-kernel-server
0 actualizados, 1 nuevos se instalarán, 0 para eliminar y 84 no actualizados.
Se necesita descargar 115 kB de archivos.
Se utilizarán 515 kB de espacio de disco adicional después de esta operación.
Des:1 http://ftp.sld.cu/debian/ jessie/main nfs-kernel-server amd64 1:1.2.8-9 [115 kB]
Descargados 115 kB en 5s (22,0 kB/s)
Seleccionando el paquete nfs-kernel-server previamente no seleccionado.
(Leyendo la base de datos ... 28996 ficheros o directorios instalados actualmente.)
Preparando para desempaquetar .../nfs-kernel-server_1%3a1.2.8-9_amd64.deb ...
Desempaquetando nfs-kernel-server (1:1.2.8-9) ...
Procesando disparadores para man-db (2.7.0.2-5) ...
Procesando disparadores para systemd (215-17+deb8u7) ...
Configurando nfs-kernel-server (1:1.2.8-9) ...

Creating config file /etc/exports with new version

Creating config file /etc/default/nfs-kernel-server with new version
Procesando disparadores para systemd (215-17+deb8u7) ...
```

Figure 6. NFS storage, 27

Now we will proceed to create the folder or directory (linux) that we are going to share with the servers to store their machines. To do this we will use the command in the following figure:

```
root@nfs:~# mkdir -p /srv/nfs
```

Figure 6. NFS storage, 28

Next we change the owner and the group, we are going to assign the folder as owner nobody and group nogroup (nobody) in order not to have permissions problems when accessing and saving. To execute the above we execute the following command line:

```
root@nfs:~# chown nobody:nogroup /srv/nfs/
root@nfs:~#
```

Figure 6. NFS storage, 29

Now we edit the exports file in the /etc/ directory to add the resources to be shared with the servers. To do this, run the following command: nano /etc/exports

Figure 6. NFS storage, 30

For a better understanding of the above configuration, I explain the file and its attributes.

/srv/nfs ------------------ Directory to be shared for the servers.

IP -------------------------- Host that will access the /srv/nfs directory.

Rw------------------------- Provides write and read permissions to the client

(servers) to the /srv/nfs directory.

Sync --------------------- Make mandatory changes to the disk before responding.

no_subtree_check--It prevents subtree checking, which is a process where the host must check if the file is actually available in the exported tree for each request.

Once the above configurations have been made, save and close the file. We create the NFS table containing the exports of the shared directory. To do this we execute the following command: exportfs -a

Figure 6. NFS storage, 31

Now we will access our server prox1.michelpress.com through a web browser, we recommend Mozilla Firefox or Google Chrome.

https://192.168.1.2:8006

Once we have logged in with our authentication data declared in the Proxmox installation. We go to the **Storage** tab, then **Add** and select the **NFS** option.

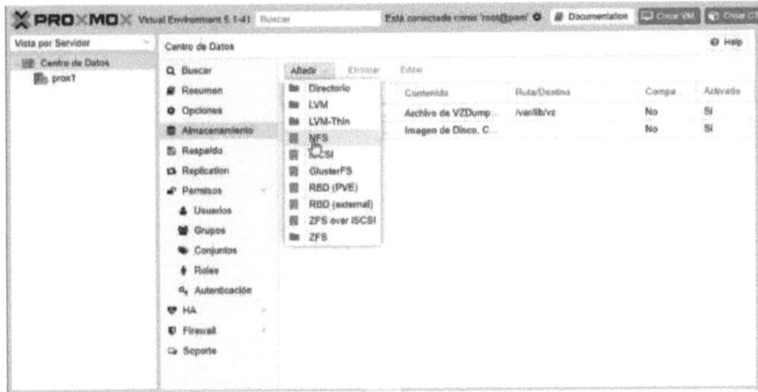

Figure 6. NFS storage, 32

In the window that opens we fill it with the data shown in the figure. But it is good when you are going to apply it you must have clear the IP of the NFS server that is going to store this server and the name that we are going to put to this NFS storage. Select the Activate box and add it.

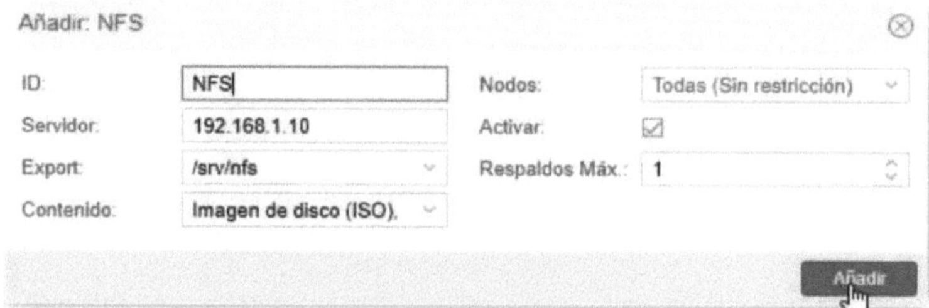

Figure 6. NFS storage, 33

In the figure below we can see that the NFS storage has been successfully added and is shared.

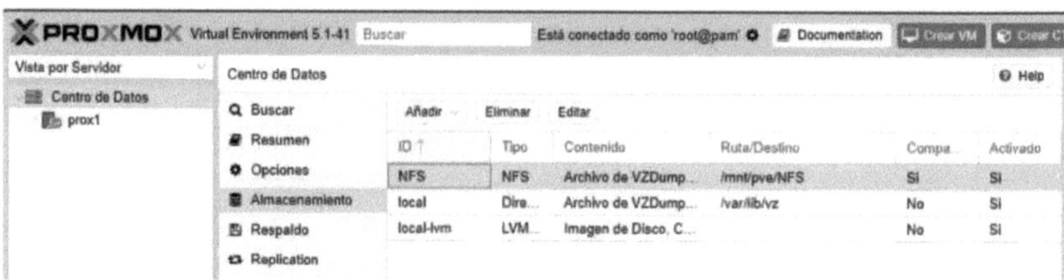

Figura 6.   NFS storage, 34

CHAPTER 6

Container Creation (CT) Debian 8 template

The first step is to upload the Debian 8 template to the NFS storage. To do this we go to *Prox1*, then to *NFS* and on the right side of the Proxmox interface to *Content*. Once in this space, select *Upload*.

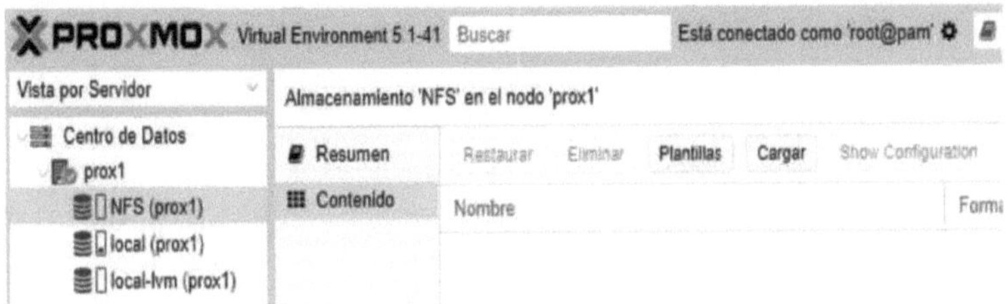

Figura 7.   Installation of Container CT, 35

Select the .tar.gz file you downloaded locally and press **Load.**

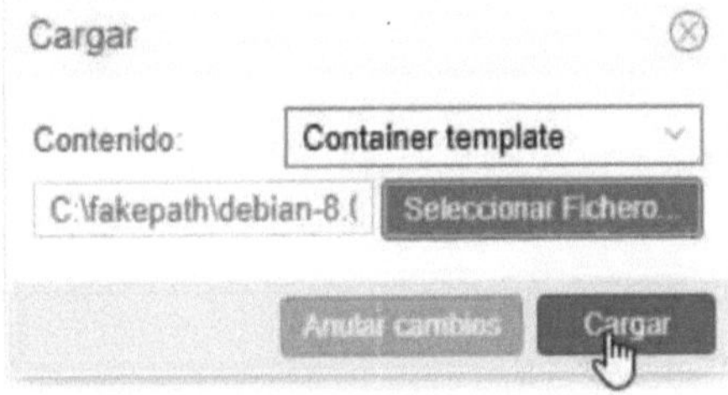

Figure 7. Installation of the CT Container, 36

The file upload process will take a few minutes depending on the size of the file.

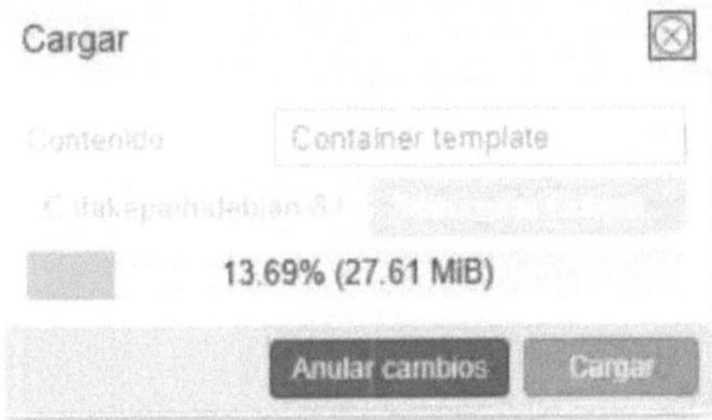

Figure 7. Installation of the CT Container, 37

At the end we will be able to have this template in Debian 8 in our shared space through the NFS server.

Figure 7. Installation of the CT Container, 38

Now we proceed to create the Container with Debian 8 for the web server where we will host our WordPress installation. We do this by clicking on the Create TC option on the top right hand side.

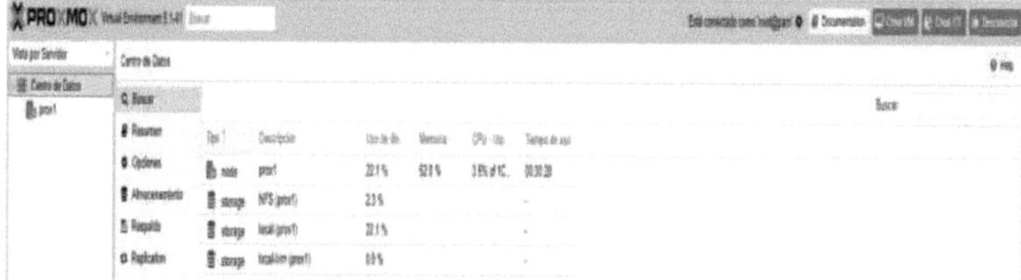

Figure 7. Installation of the CT Container, 39

We assign a name to the Container, an identifier (ID) by default the first one is 100 and the password.

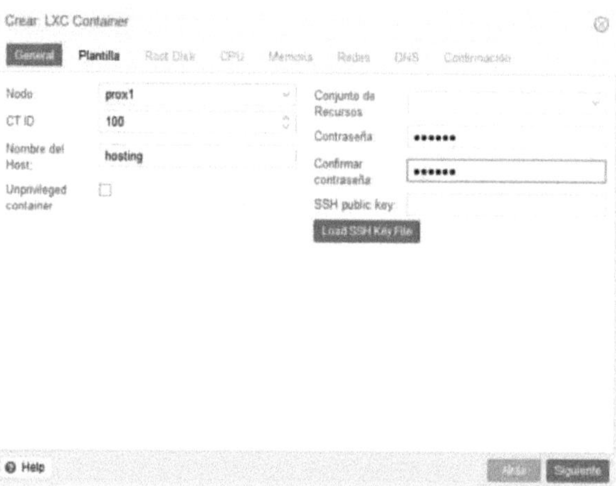

Figure 7. Installation of the CT Container, 40

In the following screens 41 to 46 we will show the procedures for assigning the storage where the template we are going to use is located, in our case Debian 8, we also assign the storage, RAM memory, microprocessors, cores, IP addressing, domain and DNS.

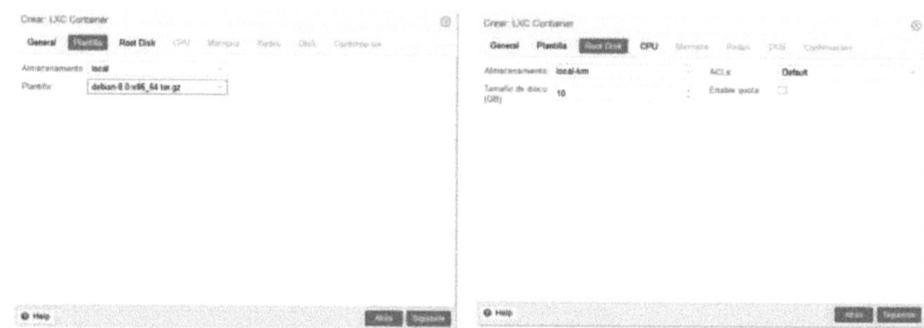

Figure 7. Installation of the CT Container, 41

Figure 7. Installation of the Container CT, 42

Figure 7. Installation of the CT Container, 43

Figure 7. Installation of the CT Container, 44

Figure 7. Installation of the CT Container, 45

Figura 7.   Installation of Container CT, 46

Once all the previous steps are done, it shows a window with a summary of all the assigned resources that our server will have in Debian 8, we press the Finished option. This will generate a window that shows the process of creation of the Container in the Proxmox, this window is not obligatory to have it open, if we close it the same one will carry out this creation in second plane.

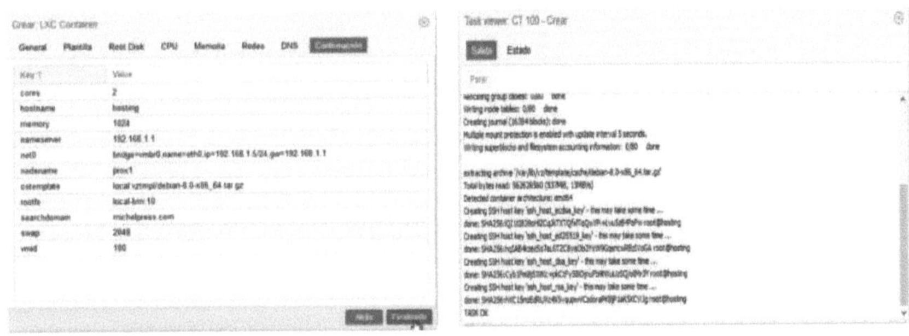

Figure 7. Installation of the CT Container, 47

Figure 7. Installation of the CT Container, 47^Q

I will now describe how the Container should be displayed once created and the power on/off state of the Container.

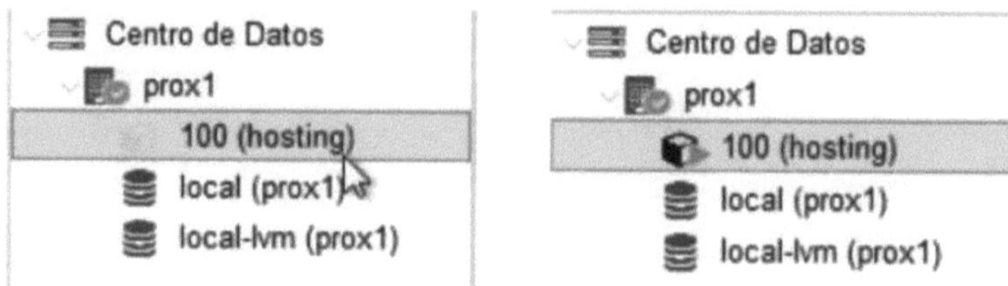

Figure 7. Installation of the CT Container, 48

Figure 7. Installation of the CT Container, 48[3]

Next, I show how to start the created Container and how to stop it, as well as how to access the Debian console in the Proxmox web interface. You can use an SSH client on Windows to access the Proxmox and the Container on GNU/Linux systems.

Figura 7.   Installation of Container CT, 49

Figura 8.   Installation of Container CT, 49[3]

Figure 7. Installation of the CT Container, 50

CHAPTER 7

Cluster creation

So far we already have the 3 nodes with Proxmox installed, the NFS server prepared to share the resources, Proxmox installations, Backups, Virtual disks, etc. So we are ready to create the cluster that will allow us to perform operations in the web interface of the prox1 (main) in all the installed Proxmox that are part of the cluster.

To start the creation of the cluster we need to prepare the 3 nodes with Proxmox. The first thing we will do is to remove the payment repository with the following command on each Proxmox server:

rm /etc/apt/sources.list.d/pve-enterprise.list

Then we will add the servers that will form the cluster in the /etc/hosts file of each Proxmox we write the name and the IPs.

```
127.0.0.1 localhost.localdomain localhost
192.168.1.2 prox1.michelpress.com prox1 pvelocalhost
192.168.1.3 prox2.michelpress.com prox2 pvelocalhost
192.168.1.4 prox3.michelpress.com prox3 pvelocalhost
```

Figura 8.   Cluster Facility, 51

```
127.0.0.1 localhost.localdomain localhost
192.168.1.3 prox2.michelpress.com prox2 pvelocalhost
192.168.1.4 prox3.michelpress.com prox4 pvelocalhost
192.168.1.2 prox1.michelpress.com prox1 pvelocalhost
```

Figure 8. Cluster installation, 52

```
127.0.0.1 localhost.localdomain localhost
192.168.1.4 prox3.michelpress.com prox3 pvelocalhost
192.168.1.3 prox2.michelpress.com prox2 pvelocalhost
192.168.1.2 prox1.michelpress.com prox1 pvelocalhost
```

Figure 8. Cluster installation, 53

We will start the creation of the cluster from the prox1.michelpress.com server, which will act as master and the other 2 will act as secondary. We must execute the following command: **pvecm create michelpress** being "michelpress" the name that will identify the created cluster.

```
root@prox1:~# pvecm create michelpress
Corosync Cluster Engine Authentication key generator.
Gathering 1024 bits for key from /dev/urandom.
Writing corosync key to /etc/corosync/authkey.
root@prox1:~#
```

Figure 8. Cluster installation, 54

To check the status of the newly created cluster, run the following command: **pvecm status**

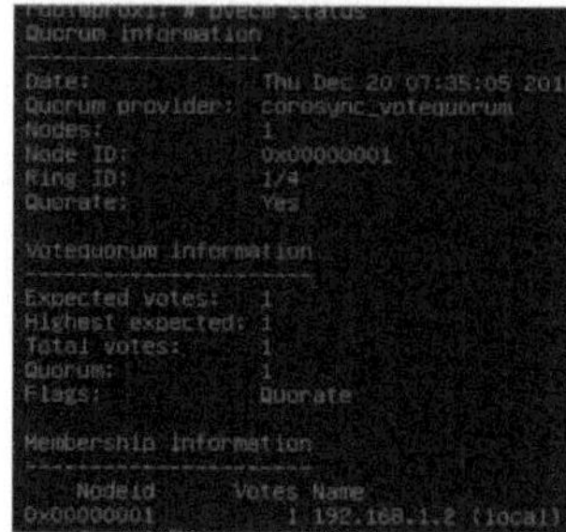

Figure 8. Cluster installation, 55

The figure above shows the cluster data and thus verifies that it has been created correctly. Now we must join the servers prox2.michelpress.com and prox3.michelpress.com to the created cluster. To do this we must execute the following command on both servers: **pvecm add 192.168.1.2** and **pvecm add 192.168.1.2** as shown in figures 56 and 57.

This command will ask us to confirm if we want to execute an SSH connection and then it will ask us for the password of the master server of our cluster.

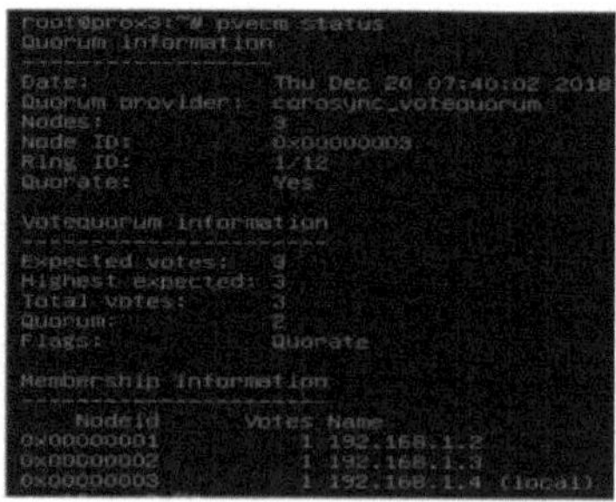

Figure 8. Cluster installation, 56

Figure 8. Cluster installation, 57

We have already created the "michepress" cluster and joined the secondary servers, now we can check from any of the 3 servers the status of the cluster with the command **pvecm status** as shown in the following figure:

Figura 8. Cluster Facility, 58

Now we can manage the 3 physical nodes with Proxmox from any of these, also the NFS shared storage is included in all the servers that make up the cluster. To visualize the previous ones we access to the web interface, in my case I will use the first node.

Figure 8. Cluster installation, 59

CHAPTER 8

High availability (HA) configuration

We are now ready to configure the management of high availability resources in Proxmox, the main reason for this document. To do so, we go to Data Centre and then to the HA tab.

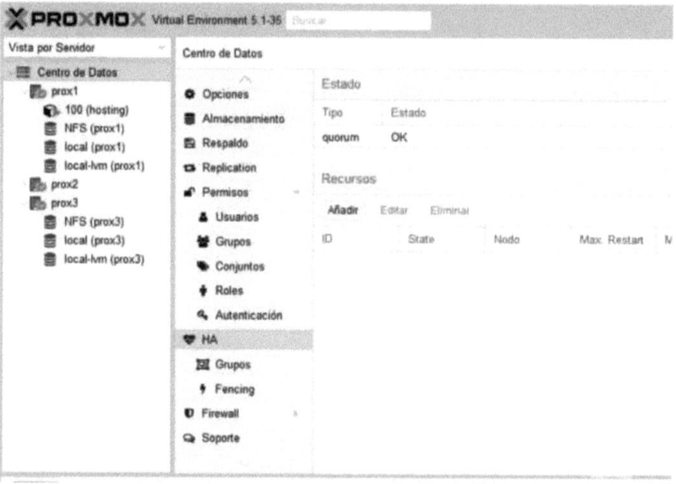

Figura 9.   High Availability Configuration (HA,) 60

Once in the HA tab, go to Groups. Click on the create option, and fill the window with the name HA and include 3 Proxmox nodes that we have installed in cluster. In addition, we activate the option "Restricted" which limits that an instance that does not belong to one of the nodes of the group is started if there are no active members of the group. Then click on "Create".

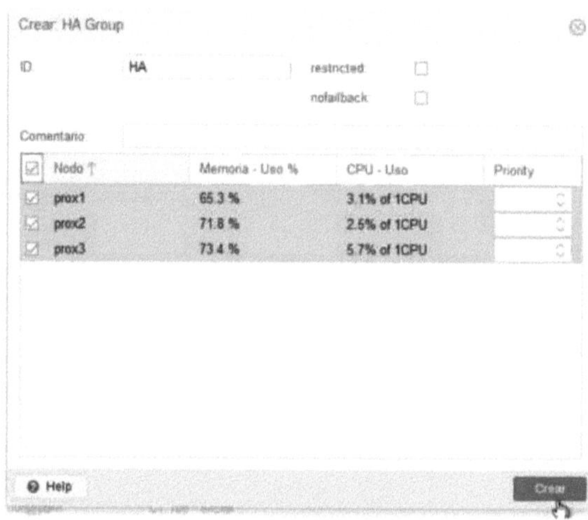

Figure 9. High Availability (HA) configuration, 61

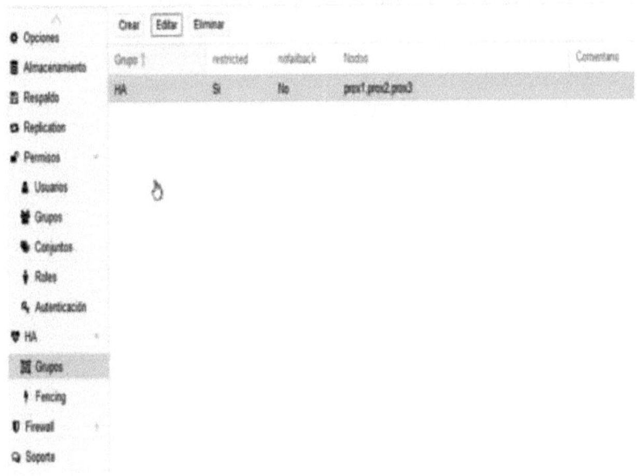

Figure 9. High Availability (HA) configuration, 62

Once the above is done, we are going to add an instance, virtual machine, lxc in operation to the group created with the name "HA" so that when there are failures in the server that contains it, it can manage the High Availability. To do this, go to Data Centre - HA - Resources and click on the "Add" option.

Figure 9. High Availability (HA) configuration, 63

Here we declare the virtual machine ID that will be in the "HA" group and that will be managed by it in case of any failure of the server that contains it, as well as the group and the comment. The options "Max. Restart", "Max. Recolate" and "Request State". Next, click "Add". When closing the window, it will show us information related to the status of the **Quorum,** the server that serves as master to manage the high availability, the asset where the virtual machine is and the other two nodes available to take over in case of failure of the active one. The above can be visualised in figures 64 and 65.

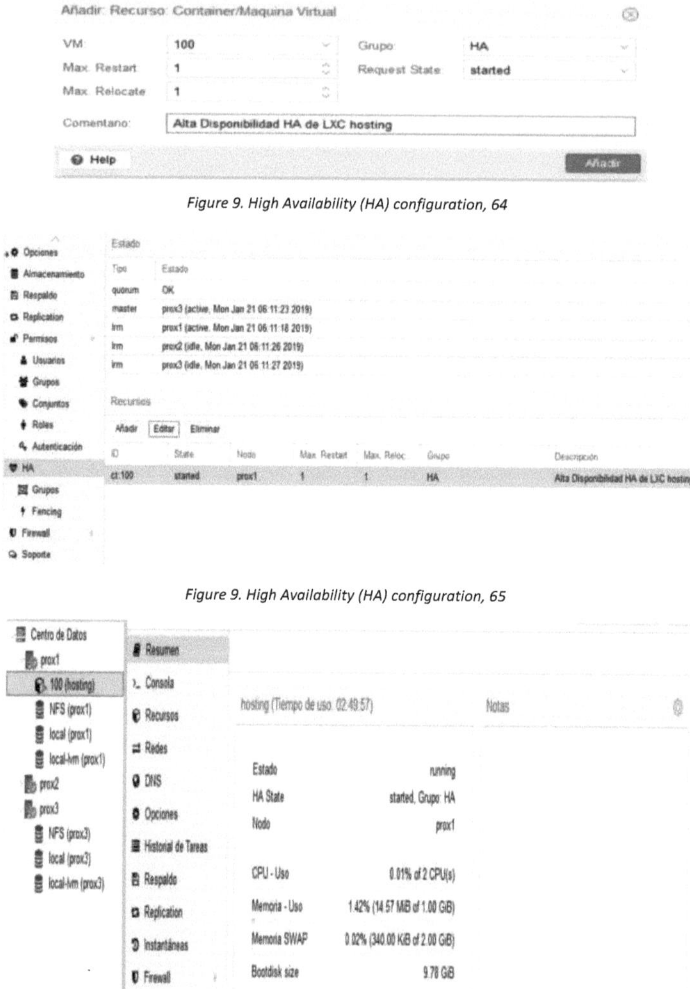

Figure 9. High Availability (HA) configuration, 64

Figure 9. High Availability (HA) configuration, 65

Figure 9. High Availability (HA) Configuration, 66

Once we have added the instance to the HA group, we will be able to see how the machine indicates that it is being managed by HA, that its status is started and it indicates the name of the group that is managing this high availability option.

The above steps are carried out for all the virtual machines contained in the proxmox server so that they can be managed by HA and, in the event of failures, automatically migrate to another server.

To demonstrate how availability works, we will intentionally shut down the prox1 node that contains the server that has the web services and we will be able to observe how the machine migrates to another server in order to continue working. To do this we will SSH into the mentioned server and execute the command poweroff as shown in the following figures: .

Figure 9. High Availability (HA) Configuration, 67

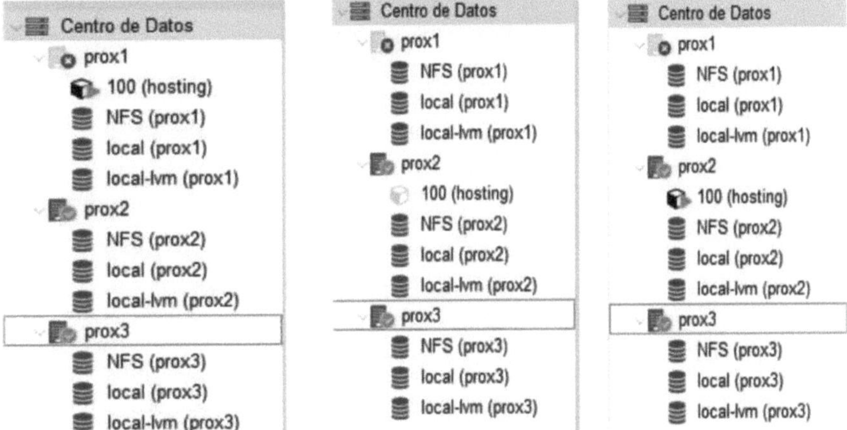

Figure 9. High Availability (HA) Configuration, 68, 69 and 70

After a few seconds, the machine migrates to another server, in this case to prox2, and then starts automatically. This process is so fast that the user who is accessing the web services does not notice the failure and the resolution process that we have configured on our servers with proxmox.

Conclusions

During the development of this project we have been able to observe how easy Proxmox allows us to install and configure a high availability cluster in Proxmox through the web interface that this environment has.

Proxmox allows you to install and configure several multiplatform systems without any possibility of incompatibility between them through virtualisation on KVM and as containers, allowing their backup and restoration in a few seconds. In addition, it manages virtual machines, storage, virtualised networks and clusters in High Availability.

Bibliographies

Gonzalo Nazareno. Department of Computer Science IES. 2017. Available at: http://informatica.gonzalonazareno.org/proyectos/201516/Proyecto.%20Cl%C3%B

Aster%20de%20HA%20en%20Proxmox%204.pdf

Digital Ocean. 2016. Available at:

https://www.digitalocean.com/community/tutorials/how-to-set-up-annfs-mount-on-ubuntu-14-04

Ali E, Susandri R. Optimizing Server Resource by Using Virtualization Technology.

Procedia Computer Science [online], vol. 59, pp. 320-325. 2015. Available at: http://www.sciencedirect.com/science/article/pii/S18770509150210188

Wikipedia. Proxmox Virtual Environment. 2017. Available at: https://es.wikipedia.org/wiki/Proxmox Virtual Environment

Estuardo Hernandez J. Installation, configuration and creation of Cluster on

PROXMOX Blog: *911-Ubuntu. 2017 .Available at:* http://911- ubuntu.weebly.com/proxmox-install-server/instalacin-configuration-and-creation-of-cluster-in-proxmox

Collective of authors. Proxmox VE Administration Guide. Proxmox Server

Solutions Gmbh. 2018. Available at: https://pve.proxmox.com/pve-docs/pve- admin-guide.pdf

Navarro Álvarez, CC. Design of a work environment for SMEs through virtualisation on Proxmox VE. Department of Telematics Engineering School

Superior de Ingenieros Universidad de Sevilla, 2016. Available in:

OchoBithaceunbyte Internet blog. 2016. Available at:

http://www.ochobitshacenunbyte.com/2016/02/17/crear-linux-containers-lxc- proxmox-4/

Wikipedia - Cluster. 2017. Available in:

https://es.wikipedia.org/wiki/Cl%C3%BAster (inform%C3%Altica]

Wikipedia - High availability cluster. 2017. Available in:

https://es.wikipedia.org/wiki/Cl%C3%BAster high availability